3-YEAR-OLDS ARE ASSHOLES

SARAH FADER

This is a work of fiction. Names, characters, places, brands, media, and incidents are either the product of the author's imagination or are used fictitiously. Any resemblance to similarly named places or to persons living or deceased is unintentional.

All rights reserved.

Copyright © 2016, Sarah Fader
No part of this book may be reproduced or transmitted in any form or by any means, electronic or mechanical, including photocopying, recording, or by any information storage and retrieval system, permitted by law.

eBook:
ISBN-10: 1-941065-18-X
ISBN-13: 978-1-941065-18-1

Paperback:
ISBN-10: 1-941065-17-1
ISBN-13: 978-1-941065-17-4

Cover Design by Shari Ryan. Edited by Susan Ethridge.

Once upon a time there lived a girl named Samantha. Samantha (or Sammy, as her mother called her) was only 3-years-old. She was bright and beautiful. She was sweet and lovely. She liked candy, shoulder rides, and television.

She spent her days trying on every single item of clothing in the house, and eating something messy while wearing each piece. The world was her oyster.

If something didn't go her way, all of existence would collapse. She couldn't even comprehend it. It was impossible. It was the way she wanted it to be, or she would destroy it. Destroy everything. In her mind, the whole universe revolved around her will.

Sammy would blow up entire planets just to get the pink jellybean instead of the white one. God love her, but she may as well have been Darth Vader.

Samantha did not give a fuck. About people's feelings. About their concerns. About what they did for her... or about anything.

Her Mommy's voice, sweet or authoritative, was merely the wind in the trees. Rules were not even suggestions. Warnings were jokes. Corrections and demands were a game of peekaboo.

One morning, by design, she awoke long before her mother. She laid there singing a quiet anthem in honor of herself, imagining all the wonderful things she could break that day. Suddenly her singing stopped. She sat up in her bed instantly, and slid to the floor, full of purpose. Winding down the hall, she heard her mother snoring.

Now normally, she'd jump on Mommy's face and scream in her ear, as this usually won her a silencing bribe of applesauce or jam. But this morning was different. There on the nightstand, like always, was Mommy's iPhone.

Glancing quickly to the left and right, she verified that no one else was awake. This was indeed the moment she'd been waiting for. Like a creeping shadow, she lifted the incredibly expensive device from its nest and stole away into the darkness.

Samantha ran into the bathroom! Quickly, quietly, she lifted the toilet lid. This was her moment. The surging arc of all she had planned and lived for. This was her Opus. The summit of her perfection. She tossed the iPhone into the toilet. Satisfaction filled her as she watched tiny bubbles escape from the phone's protective case. It lit and began to ring, but then went dark again suddenly. Thinking it must be sleeping, she gave it a blanket of half a roll of toilet paper. And then peed on it. To keep it warm.

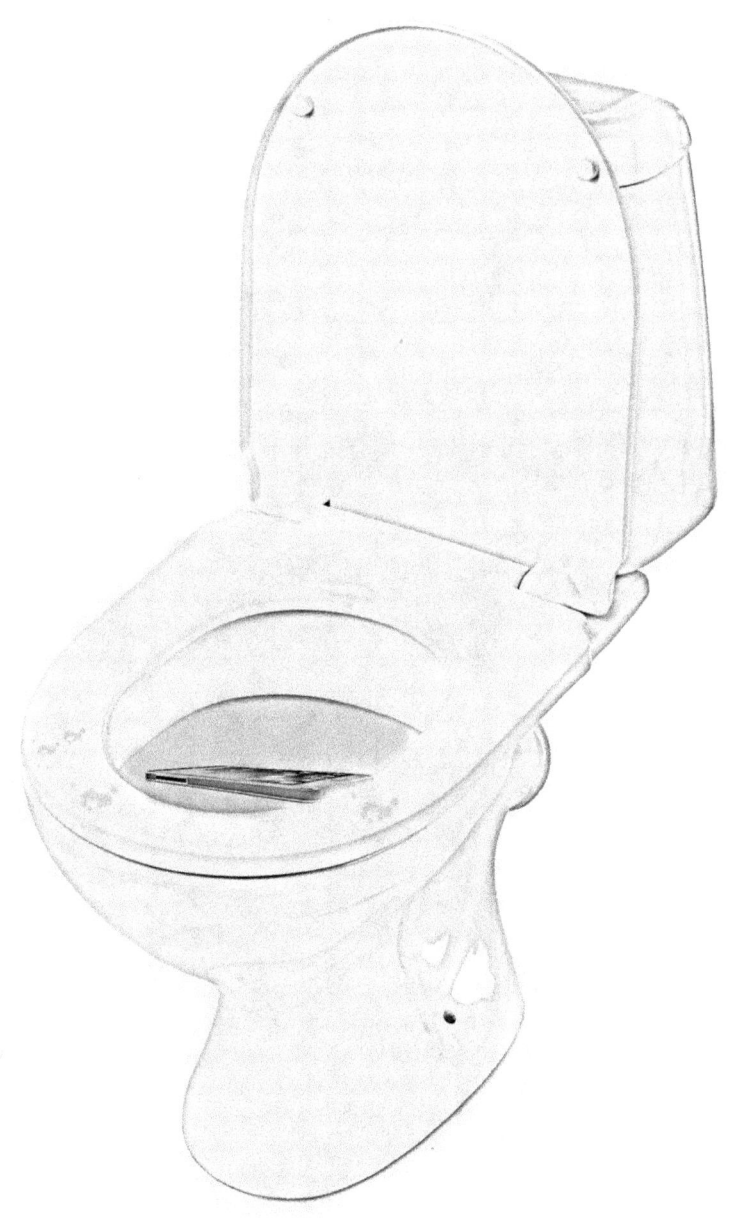

Her mission accomplished, she moved on to her secondary goal. What was behind that tiny mirrored door? Climbing deftly onto the edge of the sink, stopping only to wave at her reflection, she opened the medicine cabinet. There were so many colorful boxes and bottles in there. Some were purple, others were blue and green and pink. It was just like a birthday party!

"My birfday!" she exclaimed, knocking them all from the cabinet shelf with one swipe of her arm.

She pried the child-proof cap off of Mommy's expensive prescription pills. Pretty! Anti-inflammatories, painkillers, cold remedies, birth control pills... each bottle and box and strange plastic container had new shapes inside, and there were oh, so many colors! She would need every single one of them. This was a party, after all.

Samantha opened each container, one by one, and poured the contents onto the bathroom floor. Aside from all the lovely beads, there was pink dust from Mommy's pink container, there was goopy white slime from Mommy's white and green bottle, and there was blue sparkly goobily goop from the thing that everybody in the house used to brush their teeth with.

What a beautiful rainbow she created on the floor!

She ran into Mommy's room to wake her up and show her the rainbow. "Mommy! Good morning!" she said. Mommy grunted. She didn't want to get up. "Mommy! Good morning! Get up!" Samantha shouted. Louder this time.

"What the f-" Mommy stopped herself. Mommy then muttered something about coffee. She rolled out of bed, hardly able to stand. 3:28 teased the face of her clock, just to rub it in.

But, faithfully, she ran her finger down Sammy's cheek. "I love you baby. Why are you awake?" The cheek had some sort of powder on it, as did Sammy's pajamas, which were also wet with... something sticky.

Samantha grabbed Mommy's hand and pulled on her, until she was standing. She led Mommy into the bathroom. With each step, dread grew in the pit of Mommy's stomach.

"Look what I made Mommy! A rainbow." Mommy opened the bathroom door and saw the different colors and textures all over the floor. Mommy's jaw dropped open, cracking with tension.

"What did you do?!" Mommy exclaimed.

"Rainbow!" said Sammy, who really didn't give a shit that Mommy was in shock.

"Why!?" cried Mommy. She was angry, confused, and overwhelmed. And although she knew that making a rainbow was developmentally appropriate, she decided those particular art materials needed to be off-limits.

"Time out," Mommy said. "You are going to time out."

The tiny human who didn't give a shit was confused. All she'd wanted to do was show Mommy this rainbow. "No! I not!" said Sammy.

"Yes, you are!" said Mommy, struggling to remain calm.

So Samantha sat in a chair. She was very upset, because while she was sitting there, Mommy was cleaning up her rainbow.

Mommy fished the entire roll of wasted tissue out of the toilet with her bare hands, resigned to the dirtiness of the task.

And then she saw it. Her phone looked up at her from inside the toilet bowl.

"What an asshole," thought Mommy. But she didn't say it out loud.

She fished the phone from its watery grave, placing it on a hand towel. Mommy stared, with disbelief, in the general direction of her little vandal. She couldn't believe the level of purposeful and aggressive destruction. She silently considered the situation. "Does she hate me? Why can't I stop her from doing things like this? Am I really that bad a mother?" Worry clouded her thoughts. Her blood pressure was through the roof.

Surrendering to the task at hand, Mommy cleaned up the pills, the white goop, the blue goop, the pink powder and the green slime, all the while thinking "asshole."

While Mommy was obliterating and scrubbing the remains of the rainbow, Samantha stood up from her time out chair and escaped unnoticed.

She crept into the kitchen, pushed a chair against the counter, and opened the cupboard. Half way through pouring a box of salt out onto the counter, Sammy noticed the stovetop. She'd seen her Mommy make pretty blue lights by turning the dials. So she turned them, too. The flame rose.

There was a roll of paper towels on the counter. She looked through the roll at the flame.

The towels caught fire instantly. Sammy tossed the towels onto the kitchen counter. Dark sooty marks appeared on the countertop as the flames rose toward the kitchen cabinets.

"Mommy! Uh oh!" screamed the little girl who loved to play and explore things.

"Sammy!" Mommy shouted as she ran into the kitchen, moving her precious daughter away from the flames. Mommy tried to put out the fire, but it was too late. They ran from their home and a neighbor called the fire department, because Mommy's phone was still dead, and was now cremated.

Mommy and Sammy stood on the street corner looking at where their house used to be. There was only one thing left to do, and Samantha knew what that was. "Pancakes!" she yelled.

Mommy closed her eyes, wincing, and took a deep breath. Prying her tired eyelids open again, she saw Sammy's smiling face. Their noses were almost touching. "Fuck it," she thought. Aloud she said, "Let's go get some pancakes."

So Samantha and Mommy walked away from the smoldering ruin that was their home, and found an open diner. They sat down in a red leather booth and ordered the biggest stack of pancakes that the diner had to offer. While they ate, Mommy talked quietly and seriously about how dangerous it was for Sammy to play with the pretty blue lights, and said she must never, never do it again. Sammy tried her best to pay attention, but the syrup was so delicious and sticky.

When they were done with their meal, Mommy felt an odd sense of peace. And it wasn't just a food coma. She watched her daughter tear a small strip from their booth's worn upholstery. Everything would be okay. Mommy turned to the waiter to pay.

Suddenly, she heard a crash. She whipped around. Samantha had thrown her empty plate on the floor.

"Oops! I sorry, Mommy." Samantha looked confused.

Mommy smiled at her angel. She realized in that moment that although Samantha was capable of destroying every last shred of her sanity, she didn't mean it.

"It's okay, baby," said Mommy. "Next time, just hand me the plate when you're done. I love you."

THE END

EPILOGUE

This story was written for all you moms and dads who have your own Samanthas and Sams. It's true. Your 3-year-old is an asshole. And wonderful, and lovely, and sweet, too. You aren't alone with your conflicted feelings. But it'll be okay. It really will. Just remember to love them no matter what.

Discover more books
and learn about our
new approach to publishing
at **booktrope.com**.

www.ingramcontent.com/pod-product-compliance
Lightning Source LLC
LaVergne TN
LVHW051807080426
835511LV00019B/3429